# SILENT VOICES

HOPE HARDER

*Silent Voices*
by Hope Harder

Printed in the United States of America

ISBN 978-1-60647-608-6



www.xulonpress.com

For Phyllis –

With wonderful memories and lots of Chi Omega love,

Hope Harder

# Contents

**Dedicated to**

**The Glory of God**

# Acknowledgments

The Lord gave me the forty poems in *Silent Voices*. I wish to acknowledgment that even though I wrote them down on paper, they came from the Lord and they are totally His. To Him be all the glory. I thank Him for allowing me to be the steward of these poems.

I also want to thank my parents, H. O. "Bud" and Lucille Harder, who had faith in these poems and arranged for them to be published in 1975. Most of all I want to thank my parents for giving me a wonderful Christian home and an example of love to follow all my life.

Last, but certainly not least, I want to thank my friends and relatives who add joy to my life every day.

# Preface

The world is full of the audible voices of people and animals. I have listened to these voices and I have treasured them, but I also enjoy listening to the silent voices of the universe. Inanimate objects and entities speak, and they, too, have messages to communicate. In fact, Nature is filled with silent voices.

I deeply regret that the silent voices of the universe are usually lost in the frenzied noise of our frantic world, but I rejoice that they are vocal in the stillness of contemplation. This book is the result of my own encounter with the silent voices of the universe. I have discovered that the secret is to learn to listen for them and then to listen to them. They are always there—waiting for an audience.

# I AM SPRING

I am Spring.
Blossoms of hyacinth and daffodil
are strewn over lace to form my gown.
My hair is entwined with garlands of roses.
I dance on crocus petals
to symphonies supplied by butterfly wings
swaying to celestial rhythms.
I am the child of theYear,
joyful and hopeful.
My father was Autumn
And my mother was Winter.
Summer is my Bridegroom.
My dowry is beauty,
and my trousseau is hope.
I am Spring,
the child bride of the year.
Come smile with me on my wedding day.

# I AM SUMMER

I am Summer.
I am the Prince Consort of the Year
and the Bridegroom of Spring.
My royal diadem is bejeweled with
gardenias
and my cloak is emerald velvet.
Scepter in hand, I sit
on a throne of white camellias
and watch hummingbirds and butterflies
soar into azure emptiness.
My mother is the Sun.
In proud maternal joy,
she descends and hovers over my brow
to kiss my forehead gently.
I am Summer—
enjoy my annual reign.

# I AM AUTUMN

I am Autumn.
I rustle the leaves
and trade their green suits
for orange and amber overcoats.
I stroll across the land,
and I listen to the flowers
confess their souls to God
as they gently prepare
for Winter, rest and Eternity.
Sometimes, the leaves and I whirl to
rhapsodies
that the Wind chants.
Mostly, though, I wait in agitation
for the coming of my wife, Winter.
I warn all nature to be prepared for her
reign.
A good wife and mother,
she is frugal with her provisions.
I am Autumn.
Come, let me touch your soul
with my splendor.

# I AM WINTER

I am Winter.
I am the paradoxical season.
Usually I wear a conservative
grey and brown dress
as I perform my daily chores.
But sometimes I borrow
Snow's white lace ball gown
and I elegantly shimmer in my loveliness.
In my eagerness to see my white beauty,
I enchant all lakes and rivers.
They become mirrors,
and I avidly peer into them.
This, too, is the time I display my diamonds.
I hang them from eaves and boughs
and allow all to enjoy my frozen jewels.
Often the Sun chides me for my vanity
and forces me to watch my treasures
dissolve.
Then I am once again content
in my solemn colors
and my glorious memories.

# I AM THE OCEAN

I am the Ocean.
I wear a mantilla of white foam
and a ruffled gown of azure and emerald
velvet.
The layers of my skirt eternally vibrate
as I dance to music hummed by the Wind.
I am very methodical.
My silver-slippered feet
are punctual as they come daily
to waltz on the shoreline.
When typhoons and hurricanes intrude
on my meditation,
I become filled with fury.
Then I lay ships and men on my sacrificial
altar
and watch as their crimson presence beckons
sharks.
Later, I regain my usual tranquillity.
I am the Ocean.
Wait for me on the coast,
and I shall kiss you gently
as we rest together
on the jagged rocks of Time.

# I AM A CLOUD

I am a cloud.
An angel crocheted me out of spun Air.
I am very mobile.
Usually I skip over oceans of space
as I watch Man run through
blind alleys of Existence.
I like to drift to the rhythm of songs
written by Tranquillity
and whistled by the Wind.
Occasionally, Anger agitates the Air
with her venomous writhings.
Then I am caught in a turmoil,
and my white face wears a blackened frown.
But usually I am peaceful.
I often play hide and seek with the Sun
as I sail above men
and mentally challenge them to a game of
    tag.
I am a Cloud.
Won't you come romp with me today?

# I AM RAIN

I am Rain.
A tapestry of air
embroidered with crystal beads
is my everyday dress.
My moods are many.
Sometimes I come with tenderness,
as I baptize each flower and leaf.
But sometimes Lightning ruins my usual
calm,
as she jars Heaven and Earth
with her fork-tongued warnings.
Then I become angry,
and I strike the ground with torrential
fury.
I am Rain.
I am the mother of floods, storms and
showers.
When you see me in a gentle mood,
come waltz with me in the meadows.

# I AM A SEED

I am a Seed.
I spin and circle into Eternity.
Rich promises I hold,
and even richer bounties I contain.
I am as round as perfection
and as self-contained as the universe.
I rest and wait for God's Holy Breath
to stir life in me.
I am content.
Only Men question Divine Justice
And Eternal Wisdom.
I am a lowly seed
And downtrodden by men,
but I do not care,
for God knows,
and He cares for me,
and I am blessed.

# I AM LIGHTNING

I am Lightning.
I streak across the sky
in a silver silhouette.
Thunder, my cowardly husband,
follows me at a distance,
camouflaging his obedience to me
with earthshaking clamor.
I connect Heaven and Earth
with my jagged profile,
as I send terror into mortals.
I, Lightning, am proud of my power.
Wherever I intrude,
I leave ruin.
Twisted, broken trees are my signature.
My footprints are cores of obsidian.
I am Lightning.
Beware!

# I AM TWILIGHT

I am Twilight.
My robes are amber, gold and cerise.
I hang them on the horizon,
until I gently wrap them around my
shoulders.
Then I glide over the rim of the Earth's orb.
My family and I rhythmically
encircle the world with our beauty.
First I come to scatter the last petals of
sunshine
before the face of my mother, Night.
After Mother's ebony beauty has dissolved,
my sister, Dawn, appears to gather
sunbeams
to coronate Day in royal splendor.
The coronation completed, we rest
until our nocturnal ceremony begins again.
I am Twilight—a prologue to Night
and a prelude to Dawn.

# I AM NIGHT

I am Night.
In velvet slippers I descend
a celestial stairway.
Gently I creep down
to cover Earth in a mantle of black satin,
pinpointed with crystal lights.
I come to bring obscurity,
rest, peace, and sleep to all.
In passion I conceived Twilight and Dawn,
and like faithful twins, they accompany me
on my nocturnal pilgrimages to Earth.
I encapsulate all with ebony music.
My message is always the same:
a murmured lullaby
and a hypnotically whispered
prayer for sleep.

# I AM A LEAF

I am a Leaf
drifting through space.
Waves of air cushion my ride,
as I hover over Earth.
Infinite Time elapses,
as I fall, gently fall.
Eons and centuries of Time whirl past me.
As I fall, I watch Eternity's music
Write its score on the face of the Wind.
I descend gracefully
with innate perfection of motion and form.
I glide and float down, ever down,
through Time and Space,
until Eternity touches me
and caresses me with infinite love.
I float through a Space
whose Beginning and End is Love,
and I am content in my silent flight
toward Peace.

# I AM FROST

I am Frost.
In Autumn I coat the Earth
with my crystalline presence.
With my cold fingers
I gently wrap the ground
in my wedding veil of ice
and silently sing a hymn of praise
to Him Who made all things.
My benediction and my work over,
I press my pristine shadow
on windowpanes,
as I watch lonely people
live out their lives
of mute frustration.

# I AM SNOW

I am Snow.
The unknowing say that I am cold.
Only those who love me
know how warm I am.
I bring a blanket of virginity
to cover my beloved Earth.
Silently I come
bringing oblivion and rest.
In swirls I circle to Earth
And lay carpets of wintery flowers
over the barren ground.
I bring Silence
and a white aroma of peace.
Gently and quietly I festoon the land.
My mother was Rain
And my father was Ice.
I am Snow—I come to share
My frozen lace with you.

# I AM A MOUNTAIN

I am a Mountain.
Stolid, sturdy and alone I stand.
Others come to me for strength;
I seem unflinching and unchanging.
Only God and the Wind know how alone I
  am.
Even the trees have deserted my snow-
  capped crest.
Alone I stand—symbol of strength to Man—
and to myself—an eternal symbol of
  solitude.
Ironic, is it not?

# I AM A POOL OF CRYSTAL WATER

I am a Pool of Crystal Water.
Circles magically expand
on the mirror of my skin.
I watch them as they grow
beyond my boundaries
and radiate into space.
Eternity alone knows their limits.
I am content in my boundary of Earth,
for I know that even water has spirit,
and, thus, even I am not bound.
I will be crystalline and pure forever,
because it is the Divine Plan.
I am content in my calm state.
I feel the cloak of Silence
descend on my soul,
and I rest in eternal harmony.

# I AM FIRE

I am Fire.
My soul is an ember,
and my fingers are flames.
I dance, I jump, I forever move
as I agitate my fury.
I am Man's friend and his enemy.
I am as paradoxical as I am useful.
I am Lightning's Child,
and I am a faithful daughter.
Wherever I touch,
I leave my blackened fingerprint.
I am Fire—come not too close.
I am not yet accustomed to casual
friendships.

# I AM A RIVER

I am a River.
I slowly meander
through walls of sand.
My home is narrow,
but its roofless dimension
allows me freedom
to see God's wonders.
I forever marvel
that each grain of sand
is a microcosmic universe,
proving His Holy Existence.
As I drift slowly
toward the sea,
I know that each being
has a finite place
in an infinite pattern
and that I am in God's care.
I relax and flow smoothly,
for I am at peace
with myself and my God.

# I AM A ROSE

I am a Rose.
Scarlet, cerise, white and yellow
my wardrobe is.
Each gown is soft and fragile.
I have been called the Queen of Flowers,
and thus I am.
My court is the garden,
and the leaves are my pages.
Thorns provide me with loyal bodyguards.
The playful bee that daily flutters near
is my court jester.
My ladies-in-waiting are the proud Irises
who lift their purple heads haughtily
above their emerald gowns.
I am a Rose, Queen of Flowers.
Steal softly into my court,
And gaze upon my royal countenance.

# I AM A RAINBOW

I am a Rainbow,
gradually fading
from crimson to cerise.
Every atom of each hue
vibrates softly
to an unheard rhythm
and an unknown melody.
I am fading from human view
and gently becoming
visible to celestial eyes.
Quietly, softly, my colors whirl,
as they form symphonies and rhapsodies.
One atom of azure has recreated
    Beethoven's works,
and a particle of gold has made Brahms'.
I drift toward the circle of life,
fading into lighter colors
and softer sounds.

# I AM MEDITATION

I am Meditation.
I sit cross-legged on an amber dais,
as my mind floats over a crystal lake.
I watch water lilies
as they pray to Heaven
in their mystical splendor.
My own thoughts I string
into long ropes of pearls.
I learn valuable lessons
from all forms of Nature.
A butterfly, an old oak tree,
and a common brown field mouse
have taught me to know
Beauty, Dependability, and Vitality.
I see lessons in all life,
and I thank my Creator
for the opportunity
to learn from His Creation.

# I AM TRUTH

I am Truth.
I am transparent.
My crystal soul can not be hidden,
as I sit on a throne of mica and glass.
Rumors, gossip and slander
have attempted to injure me for centuries,
but they are only confused mirages,
when they confront my serene reality.
Men often publicly claim to love me,
but secretly they wed Deceit.
I am Truth.
Why do you look startled?
Ah, you have never seen me before—few
have.

# I AM SLEEP

I am Sleep.
Every color of existence
is woven in my gown.
As I swirl through your mind,
the colors form
a kaleidoscope of hues,
and the memory of my presence
forms the beginning of dreams.
Then I wrap my silken fingers
around your brow, and softly,
I kiss your eyes.
I sing you a lullaby,
and all your cares dissolve
in a sea of ease.
I am your servant
and your slave.
Hush, my child.
I am Sleep
and I am yours.

# I AM SORROW

I am Sorrow.
My mantle is made of tears,
and my cape is woven sighs.
I step on hearts
as I encircle the world.
Wars, Illness, and Death
have etched my face.
Once when the Earth began,
I, too, was full of joy,
but then Hatred came
and smote me with her venom.
Thus I, Sorrow, began.
My husband was Despair
and out of our union
our child, Compassion, was conceived.
All who know me
are changed by my presence.
Many become stronger—some, weaker.
The choice is theirs.
I am Sorrow.
Why do you move away, my friend?

# I AM WAR

I am War.
I am ageless, and I am eternal.
I first come quietly into men's minds.
I slip into their brains,
and I weave poisonous snares of Hate and
    Greed.
Often I march across burned lands,
waving my flag of Pillage.
Blood and Gore, my daughters, follow me
as they dutifully hold up my maroon cape.
I tread on limbs,
and I sit laughing on cadavers.
I am War.
I will come again—soon.

# I AM PEACE

I am Peace.
I walk barefoot
the path where War
in nailed boots has trod.
Millions of lives
have been ransomed
for my presence.
Men paint me carrying olive branches
and looking like a dove.
But that is not my portrait.
I am an old man burdened by the memory
of millions of other men
who have died for me.
I must endure but I am weary.
I have seen War, Pillage and Hate,
and I choose to be Peace.
Let me lean on you.
I need your strength.
I am tired, my brother.

# I AM PRIDE

I am Pride.
I have much to boast.
Men call me the "Original Sin"
but I call myself the "Original Virtue."
I rule lives and I alter History.
I am the powerful voice in men's hearts.
I am supreme.
There is beauty in my majestic stride,
as I tread into men's souls.
I ruin marriages and friendships,
and I gloat in my success.
I devour Mankind,
and I suck every atom of self-abasement
from anemic consciences.
I am Pride—arrogant, boastful, confident
    and triumphant.
I am Pride. Why do you turn away?
You know me well.

# I AM GREED

I am Greed.
I wear only silver robes.
The rustle of my metallic hems,
as I walk through men's souls,
is my favorite symphony.
Men and women worship me,
and I think I deserve to be adored.
I inspire my followers to acquire great
 wealth.
I rest on a pearl and ivory throne
with a pillow of jewels for my head.
In the Beginning, I, too, was poor.
I lusted for Happiness, and she refused me.
So I took Gold as my concubine.
The union has been prosperous,
but I still yearn in vain
for my first love.

# I AM SILENCE

I am Silence.
My voice is like white rose petals
falling on snow.
I glide in and out of noise
like light playing among shadows.
I was born the mute child
Of an Echo and a Whisper.
Gossamer and silk encircle my limbs,
and a veil of white lace
cascades from my head.
I am Silence, and I shall wrap
my cape of stillness around you
and give you my eternal peace.

# I AM A SMILE

I am a Smile.
I bring loveliness wherever I go.
I was present at the Beginning of Time.
I was hiding then
on the face of an angel,
and I overheard
the secret of Beauty.
I came to Earth the next day,
and I have conveyed the secret
to all who would accept me.
Let me adorn your face for a moment,
and I shall joyfully share
the secret of Beauty with you.

# I AM ANGER

I am Anger.
I gallop across other emotions
on a vicious gray stallion,
which my sister, Scorn, gave me.
My riding crop in hand,
I whip and flagellate the air as I pass.
My journey over, and in a calmer mood,
I practice shooting poisoned shafts
at my perpetual enemy, Love.
Finally, my energy depleted,
I wait restlessly until my satanic lover
returns from Hell
to re-detonate my soul
and re-consecrate my fury.
Then, once more, I can proudly claim,
I am Anger.

## I AM FEAR

I am Fear.
I huddle behind my robes of burlap,
as I creep slowly
toward Life's dark fringes.
I weave in and out of tragedy.
My eyes are bloodshot and swollen.
Disease, War, Poverty, and Pain stealthily
pursue me,
as I slide through the alleys of your brain.
I am Fear.
I walk on the corpses of dreams
and the skulls of departed hopes.
Hush—do you hear them?
They are following me.
Silence!
I must hide.
I am Fear,
and I am forever present
in the hearts of the multitude.

# I AM FANTASY

I am Fantasy.
I slip through the cracks of reality,
and I emerge triumphant
in your slumbering mind.
Often I creep into your daydreams
and there softly waft odors of joy
across your mind.
You can see me in a sleeping child's face,
on a maiden's smile
and in an old man's eyes at dusk.
I am Memory's consort.
I never grow old, and I am forever being
born.
Speak softly.
I do not like to be disturbed,
for I am made of mirages
and spun dreams.
Touch me and I disappear—temporarily.

# I AM PREJUDICE

I am Prejudice.
I change beauty into ugliness
and love into hate.
I am the catalyst that turns
race against race,
and brother against brother.
Usually my sister, Ignorance, precedes me
and prepares men's souls for my corrosive
seeds.
Once ingrained in a heart,
I cling with magnetic force.
I am uprooted only by God's Grace and
Knowledge.
Then I crawl out of my abode,
shrunken and withered.
But soon I find a new breeding ground.
I am Prejudice.
I remember so well the day I moved into
your heart.
We have waged many a battle—you and I.
And there are many to come.
I will see to that.

# I AM DEATH

I am Death.
I, too, was born.
Evil and Sin created me.
My mother gave me
a magic cape of myth to wear.
Around my shoulders this shroud of mystery
I have always worn.
It has worked well,
for men magnify my powers
and they mentally weave
other cloaks of myth around me.
They claim that I am victorious.
They are wrong.
Temporarily I can conquer flesh,
but that is all.
I cannot touch Spirit, Truth, Beauty, or
    Kindness.
I am described as powerful,
yet I am powerless.
Lean close, my friend,
and I shall tell you an eternal truth.
I am Death,
and only Evil, Sin, and I
can ever truly die.

# I AM REMORSE

I am Remorse.
Gray velvet veils cover my eyes.
I can see only the past,
not the present, or the future.
Leather thongs fasten me
to an eternal wheel,
circling back into agonizing memories.
I am forever writhing
over harsh words and unkind deeds.
Once Faith lit a candle,
and a small star of Light passed through my
 veils
and blessed me with a shadow of Hope.
But it soon passed away.
I am not alone, however.
Men and women continually come to me.
They whimper at my shrine,
until, refreshed with mortification,
they resume their pilgrimage to Eternity.
I am Remorse.
I alone know the eternal anguish
of futile regrets.

# I AM THOUGHT

I am Thought.
I am continually being conceived.
When Hate, Envy or Lust is the midwife,
I am shrunken and deformed.
But when Love, Faith, or Mercy attends my
birth,
I am strong and beautiful.
Sometimes I live a long life,
and sometimes I die immediately.
Often I am laid in cerebral coffins,
and there I quietly decay.
But when Truth lends me her cloak,
I can endure for eternity.
I am Thought.
Let me slide into your mind
and call it my home.

# I AM HISTORY

I am History.
Some men call me a great teacher,
but I am really a student,
watching and recording God in action.
I chisel my lessons in men's brains
and etch them on their hearts.
Sometimes I walk through the ages
with giant strides,
and sometimes I casually saunter
across centuries with a gentle step.
Wars and floods are only shadows in my
    memory.
I am conscious of minute plans,
like soft notes forming sections
of a long Infinite Symphony.
The melody, composed by the Divine
    Presence,
unfolds, century by century.
I have watched the score being written
since the beginning of Eternity.
I do not know what shall be,
only what has been.
I have faith in the Infinite Harmony.

# I AM PRAYER

I am Prayer.
I am golden filaments
uniting Man with God.
Across the universe, my atoms
link Man with the Creator
in Divine Harmony.
I come from the hearts
of the young and the old,
rabbis and nuns, Moslems and Hindus.
I dwell in the souls of men.
My existence would be peaceful,
if it were not for an impostor.
In the name of "Prayer"
often comes my enemy, Hypocrisy.
Wearing a veil of pomposity
and smirking under a cape of conceit,
she mouths long utterances in my name.
I am Prayer,
a tool of Man to reach God.

# I AM ETERNITY

I am Eternity.
I am formless,
a question in the mind of Man,
an answer in the Mind of God.
I drape my shadow over centuries,
and I whisper my echo over eons.
Years embroider my golden robes,
and seconds sprinkle my veil with diamonds.
My husband is Time,
but our union is short-termed,
for Time is limited,
and I am limitless.
I was as young as a bride,
as I shall be as a widow.
I am forever
and I am at peace.

Printed in the United States
204469BV00004B/1-42/P

9 781606 476086